MEDITERRANEAN
AIR FRYER
COOKBOOK

Heart-Healthy Mediterranean Recipes
for Cooking with Your Air Fryer

Linda Gilmore

CONTENTS

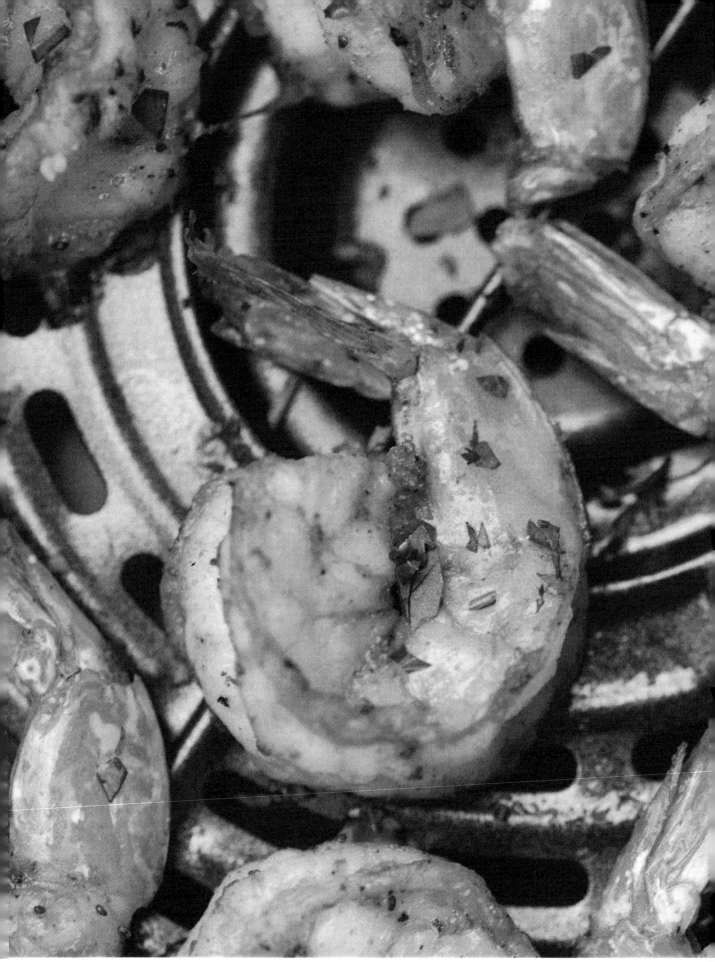

WELCOME

Are you looking for a diet that isn't just geared toward rapid weight loss? Do you want a diet that works to change your overall health and well-being? Do you want to start changing your diet so that you can maintain it for the rest of your life? The **Mediterranean diet** works differently than other 'trendy' diets because it has been used by the population that inhabits the Mediterranean region and has been shown to have **long-term health benefits such as longevity**.

Fad diets often do not consider your overall health and instead focus on one specific goal — usually weight loss. However, they are unsuccessful in the bigger picture because they are often highly restrictive and not realistically maintainable over a long period. As a result, most people will quickly regain the weight they lost on a diet as soon as they start adding back to other foods that the diet restricted. On the other hand, the **Mediterranean diet allows you to eat a wide range of foods,** making it an excellent choice for a larger portion of the population. **Anyone can find meals that they love that follow the Mediterranean diet.**

This diet allows you to reach your health goals without compromising the taste of your meals. The Mediterranean diet gives you easy adjustments you can follow, and by reading this book, you are already taking the first step. This book will provide easy recipes you can prepare; in doing so, you may not even feel like you are on a diet!

I was never conscious of my health growing up. I had countless guilty pleasures and would always go for junk food when given the option. And I never felt good. But at the time, I didn't realize that my nutrition was at the heart of all the problems that I was experiencing. I learned to love healthy foods only when one of my college roommates started cooking for our shared apartment of three. Her family was from Greece, and she was an excellent cook, especially for a college student. We would have roommate dinners, and I was introduced to cuisines I had never experienced. As I learned more about food, cooking, and nutrition, I started **incorporating more of a Mediterranean diet into my daily life**. That's when I noticeably started feeling better than I ever had. I lost some weight, but changing my diet was never about losing weight or feeling better physically and mentally.

Using an air fryer is a new way of frying food and a much better way when compared with deep-frying. This new technology is a healthy way to cook various meals — **breakfasts, poultry, fish and other seafood, meat, sides and vegetables, appetizers and snacks, and desserts** — all conveniently prepared in your kitchen.

Food made with air fryers gives the same **crispy, crunch, and flavor** as traditional fried food. Yet, it's better for you since the excess fat is eliminated because little or no oil is needed in air fryers. So, you can enjoy most of your favorite, delicious meals with an air fryer appliance. **Anything you can cook in a conventional oven, you can cook in the air fryer**. And air fryers give more cooking options than the oven. You can use them for baking or roasting without turning on your oven. Use your air fryer for cooking fish fillets — like salmon — within minutes; white or sweet potato, French fries are crispier, and the high heat treatment of vegetables renders better results.

Besides my college roommate, I didn't have many resources to help me learn about adapting to my diet. Because of that, it took me a while to fully develop my eating habits, and I did so by trial and error. I love the Mediterranean diet because it has genuinely changed my life. I have experienced first-hand how simple changes to your diet and cooking methods can change your physical and mental health. With this book, I hope to help you in your journey so that you can easily transition into your new diet and healthy lifestyle.

MEDITERRANEAN LIFESTYLE

The Mediterranean Sea lies between 21 different countries, including countries from Africa, Asia, and Europe. Because of this, the diet in this region consists of an incredibly diverse array of cultural influences. Today, the "Mediterranean diet" typically refers to a diet based on **Spain, Italy, Greece, and Turkey cuisines**.

Starting in the 1950s, researchers worldwide began studying the effects of different cultural diets on different populations' health. Specifically, heart disease became a common research point when studying alongside diets. During that time, Mediterranean populations showed significantly fewer heart disease signs. Later research on the topic has demonstrated that the Mediterranean populations' diets **help with individuals' longevity, heart health,** and other physical health benefits.

Once you start experimenting with the recipes in this book and find what kinds of foods are your favorites, you will want to eat these Mediterranean recipes instead of thinking about them as necessary for your diet. This is the central turning point in your diet journey because it's when it will begin to get easy. Starting a diet is always the most challenging part because it will be slightly unfamiliar territory. However, **finding a diet you love, just as I have, will tremendously relieve the burden**.

The longer you wait, the harder it will get, as you will grow more rooted in any unhealthy habits you engage in, consciously or unconsciously. Because you have bought this book, you are already on your way to becoming healthier! The recipes in this book will give you the tools to continue your journey.

Adopting healthy cooking techniques is vital in your journey of taking on the Mediterranean diet. When you learn how to cook in healthy and fun ways, you can **enjoy cooking and eating the food you prepare**. Trust me when I say that your body will thank you. Here are some **helpful tips** regarding small changes to transition into your new lifestyle.

- Allow **herbs and spices** to become your new go-to. This will help add flavor to your meals without adding too much salt. Experiment with different kinds of herbs and spices to use in your cooking.

- I also recommend making **lower-fat substitutions** where you can. Most foods nowadays have low-fat options. For instance, try to select a leaner cut when cooking with beef. When using dairy in your cooking, try to use a reduced-fat option. You can also easily replace butter with extra virgin olive oil in your cooking.

- The Mediterranean diet discourages foods high in unhealthy fats, such as trans fats and saturated fats. However, the diet does not restrict fat altogether. There are **healthy fats** — monounsaturated fats and polyunsaturated fats — that you can eat in the Mediterranean diet. Extra virgin olive oil, for instance, is a major staple in the Mediterranean diet that contains healthy fats.

ESSENTIAL INGREDIENTS FOR THE MEDITERRANEAN DIET

The typical Mediterranean diet includes **vegetables, olives, grains, legumes, fruits, seeds, nuts, dairy, seafood, and poultry**. Historically, these foods have appeared abundantly in the Mediterranean region, and the diet builds meals around these staples.

This diet is less about following a strictly restrictive regimen and more about making smarter choices with your eating habits. This makes the diet accessible and maintainable in the long term.

The people I have worked with on this diet have all maintained it easily. They often tell me how surprisingly easy it is to keep up because they have so many go-to recipes that are **quick, easy, delicious, and healthy**. Finding recipes, you love is the key to succeeding with a new diet. Suppose you don't love what you're eating even more than what you were eating before starting the diet. In that case, you will constantly be tempted to return to your old, unhealthy eating habits.

Foods that can serve as staples in this diet include:

- vegetables
- fruits
- whole grains
- legumes
- beans
- seafood

- poultry
- avocado
- olives
- extra virgin olive oil
- herbs
- spices

- tomato sauce
- pesto
- balsamic vinegar
- dairy
- seeds
- nuts

Foods that you will want to avoid as much as possible include foods that are heavily processed, such as:

- processed sugars
- deli meats
- soda
- saturated and trans fats
- fast food

Any food with heavy additives (these are foods that can easily be identified by looking at nutrition labels. If you see lots of ingredients that sound chemically, unpronounceable, or unfamiliar, you will want to avoid them).

A NOTE ON EXTRA VIRGIN OLIVE OIL

Extra virgin olive oil is the least processed, natural form of olive oil. It contains the most flavor as well as the most antioxidants and nutrients. It is always recommended that you choose extra virgin olive oil.

- When buying olive oil from the grocery store, look for the **harvest date** on the bottle. You will want to avoid it if it has no harvest date and only an expiration date. Try to buy the olive oil bottle with the most recent harvest date. It should also come in a darkened shade.

- It usually comes either in a **dark green bottle** or in a tin. You will want to avoid olive oil in a clear bottle. You will also want to store your olive oil away from heat and light. The pantry or cupboard makes for the perfect storage space for your oil.

WHAT IS AN AIR FRYER?

An air fryer is an amped-up countertop convection oven. It is a **kitchen appliance used to fry healthier foods like meat, potato chips, and healthier pastries**. It's a mini-convention oven used to fry foods, and it gives the same taste and texture as deep-fried foods but minus all the fat and all those extra calories.

HOW DOES AN AIR FRYER WORK?

An air fryer uses air heated to a given temperature, blows it above and around food, and converts moisture into a mist. The heated chamber allows dry heat to penetrate the food from the outside to deep inside, which gives the same crispy texture obtained from deep-fried food. A chemical reaction is caused — called the Maillard effect — a reaction between a decreasing sugar and an amino acid in the presence of heat. This reaction causes the food to change color and flavor.

The hot air inside the cooking chamber is blown in all directions, ensuring food is cooked evenly from every side.

An air fryer differs from an oven because air moves faster in air fryers than it does in a conventional oven. The cooking chamber of an air fryer is confined, so the food gets done quickly. Air-fried food is healthier than deep-fried foods because of the lower fat and calorie content. Instead of submerging the food entirely in oil, air frying just needs a little drop of oil to give a similar texture and taste like deep-fried foods. Some air fryer manufacturers boast that air fryers can reduce the fat content of fried food by up to 75%.

You can cook anything meant to taste deep-fried in an air fryer. Whatever a conventional oven can do, an air fryer can do — just better!

BENEFITS OF AN AIR FRYER

There are a lot of advantages to using an air fryer over other cooking methods. They include:

1. Quicker Meals

Since the cooking chamber is smaller than a conventional oven and the air is circulated with a fan, food gets done faster. Cooking with an oven might take 15-20 minutes to preheat, but air fryers reach desired high temperatures within minutes of turning it on.

2. Healthier Cooking

Cooking oil contains a lot of harmful constituents. With an air fryer, you can cook with little oil and often with no oil at all. You can cook onion rings, frozen fries, wings, and much more, and you will still get the same crispy texture just as if you had used oil

3. Versatility

With an air fryer, the options are endless. Compared to an oven, it fries better and healthier. It can roast, bake, broil, fry, and even grill. You can cook frozen and fresh foods, and warm leftover foods in them.

4. Space Saver

Air fryers do not take up much space compared to other kitchen appliances. All that is required is a small space on the counter, and you can quickly move or store it away if needed.

5. Ease of Use

Air fryers are easy to use: plug in, add food, select your cooking temperature, and time, and start cooking. Shake while cooking; there is no need to stir like it's done using the stovetop.

6. Ease of Clean-Up

All you have to clean with an air fryer is the basket and the pan. With ones that have a non-stick-coated pan, foods don't get stuck to it and generally easily slide off. A few minutes is all you need, and all the cleaning is done.

7. Energy Efficiency

These fryers are more efficient than an oven and won't heat your house either. If you intend to save on your electric bill or are worried about the temperature when you cook, an air fryer is an appliance for you.

MAINTENANCE OF AN AIR FRYER

An air fryer is a great appliance to keep in your kitchen, making cooking easier. Not only is it simple to use, but it also makes food very convenient. But to ensure the longevity of this appliance, some basic maintenance needs to be done to ensure it doesn't start malfunctioning or getting damaged. This includes:

- Ensure your air fryer **is not placed close to another appliance or the wall**. Air fryers require at least four inches of space around them for safety and efficiency, both above and beside. This space is needed so that vapor can be appropriately released while cooking. Putting them in a confined space might cause them to overheat.

- Make sure the **cord is in nice shape** before plugging it in. Ensure the cable isn't damaged or the wires are exposed before using your air fryer. Plugging a damaged plug into an outlet might cause sparks, leading to a kitchen fire, an injury, or even a fatality.

- Carefully **check every part of the air fryer**. Parts to note before each usage include: the frying pan, basket, and even the handle. If you locate any broken pieces, contact the store where you bought them or the manufacturer to get them replaced.

- Ensure the **air fryer is placed upright** on a flat surface before preparing food.

- Make sure the appliance is in good, **clean condition** and free from debris before you start preparing food in it. If it's been long since you last used it, check carefully, as it might have collected some dirt over time. Just in case there may be a food deposit or other dirt on the pan or basket, it is best always to clean before you start cooking.

TIPS FOR AIR FRYING

1. **Don't over pack the basket (the cooking chamber).** You might be tempted to save time by over-packing the basket, but this is counterproductive in the long term. Over packing the basket will not give the crispiness and browning needed and thus will take more time.

2. **Add a little water to the air fryer drawer when cooking fatty foods.** Adding some water to the drawer just under the basket helps to prevent oil from getting too hot and smoking. This tip is applicable when cooking any fatty foods. For example, this can be done when cooking sausage, bacon, and burgers.

3. **Use toothpicks to secure lightweight foods.** Every once in a while, the fan from the air fryer will pick up light foods and blow them around. So, secure light foods with toothpicks.

4. **Occasionally open the air fryer to check for doneness.** This is another thing that makes air fryers lovely. The drawer can be opened as many times as you like to test whatever you are cooking. This will not disturb the programmed time. Most air fryers will either pause heating as you pull out the drawer and then continue when you return the basket or continue heating and taking note of the time.

5. **Spray with oil during cooking.** If you want brown and crisp food, spritzing it with oil during cooking will give you that result. This will also ensure the food browns more evenly.

6. **Turn foods over halfway through the cooking time.** Just as if cooking on a grill or deep-frying, you need to turn foods over, so they brown evenly.

7. **Shake the basket.** Shaking the basket several times during cooking will re-distribute the ingredients and help them brown and crisp more evenly.

HAPPY MORNINGS

I don't know a more versatile dish than the frittata. It's like a quiche and an omelet at the same time. And it's great for breakfast, lunch, or dinner. I love it warm, and my husband takes it to work as a ready-to-eat meal and enjoys eating it cold. You can add anything that tastes good with eggs to it — which is almost anything. Even sweet additions are possible.

If I want to eat something light in the evening, I make a vegetable frittata (zucchini, asparagus, tomatoes, broccoli, etc.). If we're getting together as a family for dinner, I make a frittata using fish or meat (ground meat or fillet pieces). Since eggs cook quickly, make sure any toppings you add also cook quickly or are already cooked.

MUSHROOM FRITTATA

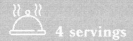 4 servings   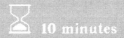 10 minutes    15 minutes

INGREDIENTS:

- 4 medium eggs
- 3 Tbsp. heavy cream
- ⅓ cup (40 g) feta cheese, crumbled
- 4 button mushrooms, diced
- 3 cherry tomatoes, halved
- 4 Tbsp. spinach, chopped
- 2 green onions, roughly chopped
- ⅓ cup (20 g) fresh parsley, chopped
- kosher salt and black pepper, to taste

STEPS:

1. Preheat your air fryer to 350°F (180°C).
2. Whisk heavy cream with eggs, salt, and pepper. Add the remaining ingredients.
3. Line a 7" baking pan with parchment paper and spray it with olive oil.
4. Pour the egg mixture into the baking pan and arrange it in the air fryer basket.
5. Cook for 15 minutes.
6. Serve with a crispy baguette.

EACH SERVING HAS:

Calories: 153, Carbs: 6.2 g, Chol: 188 mg, Sodium: 189 mg, Fat: 11 g, Protein: 8.9, Fiber: 1.7 g, Total Sugars: 3.7 g, Potassium: 408 mg

Granola is the breakfast I get up in the morning for. I adore it with milk, yogurt, smoothies, or in bar form. This Mason jar is always in my kitchen cabinet. The granola is so nutritious that I sometimes forget to eat lunch. I always make it with my kids. They are co-creators of my creativity — we choose our toppings together the day before, and on Saturday morning, we make our best granola.

I always make it with a variety of different nuts (almonds, cashews, walnuts, hazelnuts, etc.), dried fruits (dates, raisins, dried apricots, dried cherries, dried cranberries, etc.), and spices (cinnamon, nutmeg, cardamom, vanilla extract, allspice, ginger, etc.). Bon appetite!

CRISPY GRANOLA

 4 servings  8 minutes  10 minutes

INGREDIENTS:

- 1 cup (80 g) old-fashioned oats/rolled oats
- ⅓ cup (40 g) walnuts/cashews, roughly chopped
- ⅓ cup (45 g) sunflower seeds
- 1 Tbsp. sesame seeds
- ⅓ cup (40 g) almonds, roughly chopped
- ⅓ cup (30 g) coconut flakes
- ⅓ cup (50 g) dried cranberries
- ⅓ cup (50 g) raisins
- ⅓ cup (80 ml) liquid honey
- ⅓ cup (80 g) tahini paste
- ⅓ tsp. ground cinnamon
- ⅓ tsp. cardamom
- 2 Tbsp. olive oil
- a pinch of salt

STEPS:

1. Mix all the ingredients thoroughly (except the dried berries).
2. Preheat your air fryer to 350°F (180°C). Line an air fryer basket with parchment paper.
3. Pour the granola mixture into the basket in a single layer. Cook for 10 minutes, stirring every 3-4 minutes.
4. Cool completely and add dried berries. Store in a mason jar.

EACH SERVING HAS:

Calories: 610, Carbs: 59.2 g, Chol: 0 mg, Sodium: 29 mg, Fat: 39.6 g, Protein: 13.9, Fiber: 8.7 g, Total Sugars: 33.7 g, Potassium: 451 mg

Egg muffins are another versatile dish that comes to the rescue in many situations: as a nutritious breakfast for the kids before school, for my husband's meal prep for work, as a snack for keto diet followers, and as an appetizer for a party spread. They are similar to frittatas but convenient for eating on the run and as a quick snack.

They can be pure vegetarian or include meat, mushroom, or fish. I make them very quickly from leftovers in the fridge. You can reheat them in the microwave, in the oven, or in an air fryer.

EGG MUFFINS

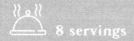 8 servings    10 minutes    10 minutes

INGREDIENTS:

- 6 large eggs
- 2 Tbsp. heavy cream
- 1 small red bell pepper (130 g), copped
- 1 small yellow onion (70 g), chopped
- ¼ cup (15 g) fresh spinach, chopped
- 6 green olives, chopped
- 3 oz. (85 g) turkey/chicken fillet, cooked and chopped
- 4 oz. (110 g) feta, crumbled
- ¼ tsp. smoked paprika
- sea salt and pepper to taste

STEPS:

1. Whisk eggs, heavy cream, salt, pepper, and paprika together in a bowl.
2. Combine the egg mixture with the remaining ingredients.
3. Preheat your air fryer to 300°F (150°C). Arrange silicon muffin molds inside.
4. Pour the muffin mixture into the silicone molds. Cook for 13-15 minutes.
5. Store the cooked egg muffins in a fridge for up to 4 days or in the freezer for up to a month.

EACH SERVING HAS:

Calories: 137, Carbs: 3.8 g, Chol: 165 mg, Sodium: 337 mg, Fat: 9 g, Protein: 10.3, Fiber: 0.7 g, Total Sugars: 2 g, Potassium: 146 mg

I am never too busy to pass up crispy toast with my favorite toppings. Morning tea or coffee with nutritious, healthy bruschetta is the best way to start the day and energize.

Instead of mashed avocado, you can use ricotta, cream cheese, or hummus. Parma ham can be replaced with sliced fish, Prosciutto, or shredded chicken. Mix and match your favorite cheeses and seasonal vegetables to make an infinite variety of nutritious and savory toasts. And, if I have time, I cook poached eggs for the top. Breakfast is the main meal of the day for me. It must be perfect.

MEDITERRANEAN TOAST

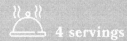 4 servings  10 minutes  15 minutes

INGREDIENTS:

- 4 whole-grain bread slices

FOR THE TOPPINGS:
- 1 avocado, mashed
- 8 green olives, halved
- 4 cherry tomatoes, halved
- 8 oz. (230 g) mozzarella, sliced
- 8 oz. (230 g) Parma ham, sliced
- 1 Tbsp. sunflower seeds

STEPS:

1. Preheat your air fryer to 400°F (204°C).
2. Arrange bread slices in an air fryer basket in a single layer. Cook for 4 minutes.
3. Place all the toppings on the bread slices and sprinkle with sunflower seeds.

EACH SERVING HAS:

Calories: 369, Carbs: 27 g, Chol: 41 mg, Sodium: 1297 mg, Fat: 20.8 g, Protein: 19.3, Fiber: 7.7 g, Total Sugars: 5.5 g, Potassium: 705 mg

Morning is the time when I have a lot of strength and energy, and I feel like I can conquer the world. That is why I am very reverent when it comes to breakfast. I wizard over the kitchen table and end up with a masterpiece on a plate or bowl. Putting together a delicious and nutritious bowl is easy, but a little preparation is still required.

I usually make a breakfast bowl from leftovers in the fridge, just reheating them in the air fryer. But if I have time, I make it from scratch. I like to use nutritious ingredients and avoid anything too heavy, which could lead to a bad breakfast and spoil my whole day. I always add high-protein ingredients like chicken, mushrooms, falafel, eggs, or fish. Vegetables and greens make up the rest. Serve with your favorite toasted Italian bread. Let's make it together!

BREAKFAST BOWL

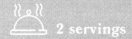 2 servings    10 minutes    8 minutes

INGREDIENTS:

- ⅓ cup (45 g) sunflower seeds
- 5 falafels
- 2 cherry tomatoes, halved
- 1 tsp. Italian seasoning
- ½ avocado, coarsely chopped
- 6 green olives
- lettuce leaves, chopped
- 2 Tbsp. tahini dressing
- 1 cup (240 g) hummus/baba ganoush
- 1 poached egg
- sea salt
- extra virgin olive oil

STEPS:

1. Preheat your air fryer to 370°F (190°C).
2. Toss eggplant slices and tomatoes with olive oil, salt, and Italian seasoning.
3. Arrange them in an air fryer basket in a single layer. Cook for 7-8 minutes.
4. Assemble the bowl. Add air-fried eggplant, tomato halves, lettuce leaves, falafel, chopped avocado, and olives. Drizzle with tahini dressing.
5. Serve with hummus, air-fried chicken slices, and poached egg.

EACH SERVING HAS:

Calories: 655, Carbs: 49 g, Chol: 95 mg, Sodium: 1192 mg, Fat: 43.8 g, Protein: 22.3, Fiber: 14.7 g, Total Sugars: 6.5 g, Potassium: 1282 mg

Of course, this rarely happens, but French toast is always helpful if we run out of dessert at home. It is quick and easy to make, especially with an air fryer. You have a delicious and nutritious dessert in 10 minutes, which is perfect as a wholesome breakfast. I like to eat mine hot with a flavored latte.

You can use any berries, fruits, or nuts for topping, and the honey can be replaced with caramel or berry syrup. You can serve French toast on Sunday morning with a scoop of vanilla ice cream.

FRENCH TOAST

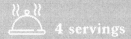 4 servings   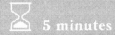 5 minutes    10 minutes

INGREDIENTS:

- 4 thick (¾") slices brioche/baguette/challah
- 4 medium eggs
- ⅔ cup (160 ml) whole milk
- 1 tsp. vanilla extract
- 1 Tbsp. honey
- ½ tsp. cinnamon

FOR THE TOPPINGS:
- blue cheese, grilled
- caramelized pears
- pistachios, chopped

STEPS:

1. Whisk together milk, eggs, cinnamon, honey, and vanilla extract.
2. Preheat your air fryer to 350⁰F (177⁰C).
3. Dip your bread slices into the mixture and place them in an air fryer basket. Cook for 6-10 minutes until golden, flipping halfway through.
4. Spread blue cheese on the toasts. Top with caramelized pear slices and sprinkle with chopped pistachios. Serve with liquid honey.

EACH SERVING HAS:

Calories: 262, Carbs: 23.9 g, Chol: 174 mg, Sodium: 206 mg, Fat: 14.1 g, Protein: 11 Fiber: 1.7 g, Total Sugars: 11.1 g, Potassium: 212 mg

SNACKS & APPETIZERS

Roasted Almonds	35
Baba Ganoush	37
Falafel	39
Stuffed Mushrooms	41
Romesco Sauce	43

If you love roasted almonds, you'll love these fried almonds, too. We always have these sweet, crunchy nuts on hand at home. Our family eats them both as a snack and as an addition to salads, breakfast porridge, desserts, and baked goods. Also, my kids take some when they visit friends, putting them in pretty little jars as gifts.

Before putting the almonds in the fryer, I mix them with various coatings. In 5 minutes, the flavorful, crunchy almonds are ready. Their flavor after air frying is brighter than raw. Of course, this can all be done in a skillet as well.

Before storing the almonds, cool them completely.

Almonds contain a huge amount of healthy fats, plant protein, and microelements, making this treat an excellent supplement for vegans as well as paleo and keto followers.

Other nuts can be toasted using the same recipe: try pecans, walnuts, and cashews.

ROASTED ALMONDS

 1 cup/4 servings   2 minutes   5 minutes

INGREDIENTS:

- 1 cup (130 g) raw almonds/pecan/ walnuts/cashew

FOR SWEET ALMONDS (optional):
- sugar
- cinnamon
- pumpkin pie spice

FOR SAVORY ALMONDS (optional):
- herbs
- nutmeg
- oriental spices/curry
- onion/garlic powder
- chili powder
- olive oil/melted butter/coconut oil

STEPS:

1. In a small bowl, mix almonds with your favorite seasoning.
2. Place them in a single layer in an air fryer basket and fry at 350°F (180°C) for 5 minutes.
3. Don't forget to shake the basket 2 times during cooking.
4. Cool completely before serving.
5. These nuts can be stored in a jar for 1-2 months.

EACH SERVING HAS:

Calories: 149, Carbs: 8.9 g, Chol: 0 mg, Sodium: 0 mg, Fat: 12 g, Protein: 5 Fiber: 3 g, Total Sugars: 4 g, Potassium: 174 mg

BABA GANOUSH

Baba Ganoush is a famous Lebanese eggplant dish. It is similar to hummus but based on eggplants instead of chickpeas. It is loved even by those who do not generally like eggplant. It is a nutritious appetizer due to tahini, a paste made from sesame seeds. Before you can mash the eggplants, you must soften them. You can do this by frying it in a skillet, baking in the oven, or even grilling. I suggest you air fry them. To keep the dip from being watery, squeeze the excess liquid out of the cooked eggplant before proceeding with the recipe.

I like to pair this rich flavor with toasted whole-grain bread, flatbread, pita chips, crackers, raw bell pepper wedges, or cucumber slices. I use red pepper flakes, crumbled feta cheese, or parsley sprigs for a garnish.

BABA GANOUSH

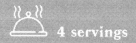 4 servings   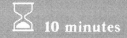 10 minutes    20 minutes

INGREDIENTS:

- 1 medium eggplant (1 lb./450 g), cut lengthwise
- 1 Tbsp. vegetable oil
- 2 Tbsp. tahini paste
- 2 tsp. fresh lemon juice
- 2 garlic cloves, peeled
- a pinch of sea salt
- a pinch of nutmeg
- 1 tsp. fresh parsley, chopped

STEPS:

1. Wrap garlic clove in aluminum foil.
2. Make several holes in the eggplant skin using a fork.
   Place the eggplant halves cut side down and the foil-wrapped garlic in the air fryer basket. Cook in the preheated air fryer at 400°F (200°C) for 15-20 minutes until the eggplant is golden brown.
3. Peel and chop the cooled eggplant. Let it drain for 5 minutes.
4. Put drained eggplant with all other ingredients (except parsley) into the food processor. Make a coarse puree.
5. Store baba ganoush in the fridge. Serve with feta cheese and chopped parsley.

EACH SERVING HAS:

Calories: 106, Carbs: 8.9 g, Chol: 0 mg, Sodium: 12 mg, Fat: 7.7 g, Protein: 2.5 Fiber: 4.8 g, Total Sugars: 3.6 g, Potassium: 304 mg

FALAFEL

In this recipe, I adapted this incredibly delicious Arabian dish for cooking in an air fryer. It's like a device made for falafel. We cook with minimal oil, and even vegans are satisfied with its nutritional value.

I use an ice cream scoop, which is just the right size, to form nice, even balls. I always cook with dry chickpeas and soak them myself. If you use canned chickpeas, the mixture is too moist. Getting the right texture is essential so the balls to keep their shape. If the balls fall apart, you can add 1-2 tablespoons of chickpea flour or any other flour.

You can serve them with pita bread or as a snack with baba ganoush, tahini sauce, or hummus.

FALAFEL

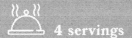 4 servings   10 minutes (plus one day for soaking chickpeas and 1 hour for refrigerating)    10 minutes

INGREDIENTS:

- 2 cups (400 g) dried chickpeas
- 4 garlic cloves, minced
- 1 small red onion (50 g), chopped
- ¾ cup (45 g) fresh parsley, chopped
- ½ cup (30 g) fresh cilantro, chopped
- 1 Tbsp. ground coriander
- 1 Tbsp. ground cumin
- 1 tsp. sea salt
- ½ tsp. ground white pepper
- 1 tsp. red pepper flakes
- 1 tsp. baking powder

STEPS:

1. Soak chickpeas in a large bowl of water for 24 hours. Drain well. The chickpeas should be softened. The chickpeas must become softer but not as soft as cooked chickpeas.
2. Blend the drained chickpeas, red onion, garlic, spices, and herbs, baking powder, and salt in a food processor.
3. Let the mixture rest in the fridge for 1 hour.
4. Shape small balls with your hand or using an ice cream scoop. Spray the balls and the air fryer basket with olive oil.
5. Arrange falafel balls in the basket in a single layer. Cook at 400°F (204°C) for 10 minutes, flipping halfway through.
6. Serve in a pita pocket with tahini sauce, air-fried bell peppers, and red onion rings.

EACH SERVING HAS:

Calories: 390, Carbs: 65 g, Chol: 0 mg, Sodium: 39 mg, Fat: 6.7 g, Protein: 20.5 Fiber: 18.8 g, Total Sugars: 11.6 g, Potassium: 1179 mg

STUFFED MUSHROOMS

Everyone loves appetizers because they are bite-sized, and you don't notice how many you are eating — they are incredibly tasty, after all. Stuffed mushrooms are versatile because they can be filled with any kind of stuffing: different types of cheese, bell peppers, crabmeat, pepperoni, and a variety of seasonings.

These stuffed mushrooms can be prepared in advance and then stored in the refrigerator for 2 to 3 days. You can reheat them again in the air fryer for 3 to 4 minutes.

STUFFED MUSHROOMS

 16 mushrooms   10 minutes   26 minutes

INGREDIENTS:

- 16 mushrooms (1 lb./450 g) (like cremini mushrooms), rinsed and dried
- ¼ cup (60 g) sun-dried tomatoes, chopped
- ½ cup (75 g) breadcrumbs
- 1 green onion, chopped
- 4 oz. (110 g) cream cheese
- 4 oz. (110 g) parmesan, shredded

STEPS:

1. Cut stems from the mushrooms and scoop out the center. Chop them finely.
2. Mix the chopped stems, sun-dried tomatoes, breadcrumbs, cream cheese, shredded cheese, and green onion.
3. Fill the mushrooms with the stuffing.
4. Arrange mushrooms in a single layer. Cook in the air fryer preheated to 400°F (204°C) for 6 minutes.
5. Your perfect Mediterranean appetizer is ready.

EACH SERVING HAS:

Calories: 72, Carbs: 5 g, Chol: 12 mg, Sodium: 121 mg, Fat: 4.2 g, Protein: 4.5 Fiber: 0.8 g, Total Sugars: 0.9 g, Potassium: 119 mg

ROMESCO SAUCE

This rich Spanish sauce is trendy all over the world. It consists of the most beloved Mediterranean ingredients: roasted bell peppers, sun-dried tomatoes, garlic, toasted nuts, and Italian seasoning. Sun-dried tomatoes make for a rich flavor, but they can be substituted with canned tomatoes or fresh ripe tomatoes.

Serve the sauce or dip with fried or fresh vegetable wedges, smoked meat or poultry, and pita bread.

ROMESCO SAUCE

 4 servings 10 minutes  50 minutes

(plus 6-8 hours of soaking time)

INGREDIENTS:

- 1 big red bell pepper (150 g), diced
- ¾ cup (100 g) toasted/air-fried almonds/walnuts/hazelnuts
- ¾ cup (100 g) sun-dried tomatoes
- ¼ cup (60 ml) olive oil
- 4 garlic cloves
- ½ lemon, juiced
- 1 tsp. smoked paprika
- ½ tsp. cayenne pepper
- ½ tsp. sea salt
- ½ tsp. sugar

FOR SUN-DRIED TOMATOES:

- 10 ripe cherry tomatoes, quartered
- 1 tsp. olive oil
- 1 tsp. Mediterranean seasoning
- tsp. sea salt and black pepper
- olive oil for soaking

STEPS:

FOR SUN-DRIED TOMATOES:

1. Toss tomatoes with olive oil, seasoning, salt, and pepper. Place them in a single layer in a grill pan/cake pan.
2. Put the pan with the tomatoes into the air fryer preheated to 240°F (115°C). Cook for 30-40 minutes, checking every 10 minutes.
3. Put the cooked tomatoes into a glass jar and add olive oil. Soak for 6-8 hours.

FOR THE SAUCE:

4. Sprinkle bell peppers with olive oil and salt. Wrap garlic cloves in a piece of foil.
5. Preheat your air fryer to 360°F (180°C). Arrange bell peppers and wrapped garlic in a fryer basket and cook for 10 minutes.
6. Add all the ingredients for Romesco sauce to a food processor and blend into a smooth paste.
7. Store in a fridge for 7-8 days or in the freezer for up to 5 months.

EACH SERVING HAS:

Calories: 303, Carbs: 10 g, Chol: 0 mg, Sodium: 3 mg, Fat: 29.7 g, Protein: 4.6 Fiber: 3.8 g, Total Sugars: 4 g, Potassium: 324 mg

VEGETABLES

I don't just cook this warm Mediterranean salad (or side dish) every summer, I look forward to summer to make these colorful and delicious roasted vegetables. They're quick and easy to make, and they keep in the fridge for days. You can pick any mix of vegetables you want, but the classic version is my favorite. You can even substitute all the summer vegetables for root vegetables, increasing the cooking time a bit. Simple organic vegetables make an excellent ensemble. According to the basic cooking principles, the vegetables are cut into roughly equal-sized pieces.

Roasted vegetables are great as a garnish for air-fried salmon and chicken thighs or as toppings for pizza or bruschetta.

ROASTED VEGETABLES

 4 servings 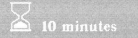 10 minutes 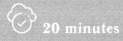 20 minutes

INGREDIENTS:

- 1 small eggplant (300 g), diced or cubed
- 1 small zucchini (140 g), diced or cubed
- 3 cherry tomatoes, halved
- 2 bell peppers (300 g), cut into wedges
- 1 red onion (70 g), quartered
- 4 big garlic cloves, halved
- 1 cup (100 g) mushrooms, halved
- ½ tsp. red pepper flakes
- 1 tsp. Mediterranean herbs
- ¼ tsp. sea salt
- 3 Tbsp. olive oil

STEPS:

1. Preheat your air fryer to 375°F (190°C).
2. Toss vegetables with olive oil, herbs, spices, and salt.
3. Place the vegetables (except the tomatoes) in a basket in a single layer. Depending on the size of your device, you may need to cook them in two stages.
4. Cook for 5 minutes. Next, add the tomatoes, stir them into the vegetables, and cook for another 5 minutes.
5. Serve with cubed feta cheese.

EACH SERVING HAS:

Calories: 186, Carbs: 19 g, Chol: 0 mg, Sodium: 84 mg, Fat: 11.2 g, Protein: 4 Fiber: 7.2 g, Total Sugars: 11 g, Potassium: 794 mg

My kids quite reasonably believe that the best way to cook young potatoes is to air fry them. To get potatoes with a crispy outside and tender inside, we borrowed this recipe from Greece. Marjoram and rosemary can be substituted for the Greek seasoning blend.

Before I met this device, I thought that the easiest and most elegant way to cook potatoes was by roasting, but with the air fryer, they become kind of caramelized. I also use this method to cook caramelized baby carrots (with orange juice, cinnamon, brown sugar, and red pepper), or beetroots. Crumbled feta and diced olives are complementary garnish.

CRISPY GREEK POTATOES

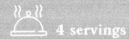 4 servings    5 minutes   20 minutes

INGREDIENTS:

- 1 lb. (450 g) baby potatoes, halved
- 2 Tbsp. olive oil
- 1 Tbsp. fresh lemon juice
- 1 Tbsp. lemon zest
- 3 garlic cloves, crushed
- 1 tsp. dried rosemary
- 1 tsp. dried marjoram
- a pinch of sea salt, and pepper
- 1 Tbsp. fresh dill, chopped, for garnish

STEPS:

1. Preheat your air fryer to 400°F (204°C).
2. Pat your potatoes dry and toss in herbs, lemon juice, zest, garlic, and olive oil. Spread them in a single layer in an air fryer basket.
3. Cook for 15 minutes, shaking the basket halfway through, until light golden brown.
4. Garnish with freshly chopped dill.
5. Pair Greek potato with pork chops, white fish, or creamy mushrooms.

EACH SERVING HAS:

Calories: 134, Carbs: 16 g, Chol: 0 mg, Sodium: 14 mg, Fat: 7.2 g, Protein: 3.3 Fiber: 3.2 g, Total Sugars: 0.2 g, Potassium: 518 mg

This Lebanese recipe has a few subtleties when cooking in the air fryer. You need to pick peppers in such a shape that they can stand stably in the basket and not fall off. They must also be large enough to hold a lot of stuffing. For the best results, cook the peppers in the microwave for 1 to 2 minutes before finishing in an air fryer.

For a vegetarian option, you can replace the meat with roasted mushrooms. And if you replace white rice with cauliflower rice, even keto followers can enjoy it. If you store the stuffed peppers in the fridge, you can reheat them in the air fryer, oven, or microwave.

STUFFED BELL PEPPERS

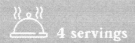 4 servings  10 minutes  40 minutes

INGREDIENTS:

- 4 bell peppers (600 g), wide and short
- 1 lb. (450 g) ground beef/turkey
- 1 cup (250 g) jasmine rice/quinoa/bulgur, cooked
- 1 (15 oz./425 g) can of crushed tomatoes
- 1 small onion (50 g), chopped
- 1 garlic clove, minced
- 1 tsp. dried oregano
- 1 tsp. dried thyme
- ¼ tsp. nutmeg
- ½ tsp. allspice
- ¼ tsp. paprika
- ¼ tsp. sea salt
- ½ Tbsp. olive oil
- 1 cup (120 g) Mozzarella cheese, grated

STEPS:

FOR THE FILLING:

1. In a large skillet, lightly fry chopped onion and garlic in olive oil until they soften.

2. Add ground meat and cook for 5-7 minutes.

3. Remove meat from the heat and add rice, seasonings, ½ cup of grated cheese, crushed tomatoes, and salt.

FOR THE PEPPERS:

4. Cut the tops off the peppers and remove everything from the inside. Fill them with stuffing.

5. Preheat the air fryer to 360°F (180°C).

6. Arrange peppers in the basket, right side up. Cook for 12 minutes. Sprinkle ½ cup of cheese on top. Cook for another 2-3 minutes.

7. Serve warm with fresh basil.

EACH SERVING HAS:

Calories: 393, Carbs: 31.5 g, Chol: 106 mg, Sodium: 334 mg, Fat: 11 g, Protein: 42 Fiber: 5.9 g, Total Sugars: 12.8 g, Potassium: 724 mg

Although you can buy asparagus year-round, I like to eat it in season. It can be fried, boiled, or baked, and it cooks in just a few minutes. If you cook it even a little too long, it gets tough, and our goal is to get soft stalks with a little crunch. I love asparagus specifically for its tenderness and nutritional value.

My husband likes to serve it as a side dish to air-fried salmon, white fish, or Greek chicken thighs. It pairs well with lemon juice and cheese sauces. As a bonus, the Tahini sauce in the recipe can be used for other dishes and as a salad dressing.

ASPARAGUS WITH TAHINI SAUCE

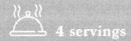 4 servings 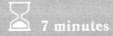 7 minutes  7 minutes

INGREDIENTS:

- 1 lb. (450 g) fresh asparagus
- 1 Tbsp. sesame seeds/feta cheese
- 1 Tbsp. olive oil
- a pinch of sea salt, and black pepper

FOR THE TAHINI SAUCE:

- 3 Tbsp. tahini
- 1 lemon, zest, and juice
- 1 garlic clove, crushed
- 2 Tbsp. water
- 2 Tbsp. sesame oil
- ½ tsp. sea salt
- ¼ tsp. paprika

STEPS:

1. Cut off the hard, woody ends of the asparagus and peel away any tough parts. Sprinkle with olive oil, salt, and pepper.
2. Preheat your air fryer to 380°F (195°C). Arrange asparagus in the basket in a single layer. Cook for 7 minutes until it crisp-tender.
3. Blend all ingredients for the tahini sauce.
4. Drizzle asparagus with tahini sauce and sprinkle with sesame seeds.

EACH SERVING HAS:

Calories: 200, Carbs: 10.5 g, Chol: 0 mg, Sodium: 17 mg, Fat: 17.7 g, Protein: 5.2 Fiber: 5 g, Total Sugars: 2.2 g, Potassium: 330 mg

I love this simple salad with lightly caramelized zucchini and lots of fresh herbs. Zucchini can be pan-fried, baked in the oven, or grilled. Air frying allows you to cook with very little oil and save all the healthy trace minerals.

When I would find myself with a lot of zucchini, I used to make a filling, stuff them and bake them for a long time, and then sprinkle them with cheese. But when I came across this salad and adapted it to the air fryer, I forgot about stuffed zucchini. You, too, will appreciate this sweet and garlicky flavor next to pork chops, steak, or lamb.

ZUCCHINI SALAD

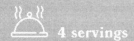 4 servings   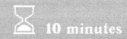 10 minutes   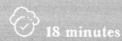 18 minutes

INGREDIENTS:

- 1 lb. (450 g) / 2 medium zucchini, diced or cubed
- a pinch of salt and pepper
- ½ tsp. cumin
- 2 Tbsp. olive oil, divided
- ½ lemon, juiced
- 1 garlic clove, minced
- ½ cup (30 g) fresh parsley, chopped
- 1 Tsp. fresh basil, chopped
- ½ cup (60 g) feta cheese, crumbled

STEPS:

1. Preheat your air fryer to 425°F (220°C).
2. Toss zucchini with salt, pepper, cumin, and 1 tablespoon olive oil.
3. Place zucchini in an air fryer basket in a single layer. Cook for 14-18 minutes, flipping halfway through.
4. Mix air-fried zucchini, lemon juice, garlic, and chopped herbs in a bowl.
5. Sprinkle with crumbled feta cheese.

EACH SERVING HAS:

Calories: 122, Carbs: 4.9 g, Chol: 13 mg, Sodium: 183 mg, Fat: 10.7 g, Protein: 3.7 Fiber: 1.4 g, Total Sugars: 2.5 g, Potassium: 323 mg

There are a few ways to get crispy cabbage, and air frying is the best. Almost any kind of cabbage can be cooked this way. Simply cut it into desired pieces, salt and season it, and air fry. Garlic tahini sauce or honey mustard sauce is a perfect accompaniment. Sprinkle the top with sesame seeds, shredded cheese, or a coarsely ground nut mix.

I love pairing crispy cabbage wedges with juicy pork chops. You'll change your mind about cabbage once you try this recipe.

VEGETABLES

CRISPY CABBAGE

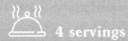 4 servings 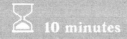 10 minutes  18 minutes

INGREDIENTS:

- 1 head green/red cabbage (800 g), cut into wedges/steaks
- avocado oil spray
- sea salt
- 1 tsp. onion powder
- 1 tsp. garlic powder

FOR THE TAHINI SAUCE:
- 3 Tbsp. tahini
- 1 lemon (90 g), zest and juice
- 1 garlic clove, crushed
- 2 Tbsp. water
- 2 Tbsp. sesame oil
- ½ tsp. sea salt
- ¼ tsp. paprika
- 2 Tbsp. green onion, chopped

STEPS:

1. Spray cabbage wedges with avocado oil and season with sea salt, garlic powder, and onion powder.
2. Preheat your air fryer to 400°F (204°C). Arrange cabbage wedges in a basket in a single layer. Cook for 18 minutes, flipping halfway through.
3. Combine all ingredients for the tahini sauce.
4. Serve air-fried cabbage with tahini sauce.

EACH SERVING HAS:

Calories: 189, Carbs: 17.4 g, Chol: 0 mg, Sodium: 47 mg, Fat: 13.7 g, Protein: 4.9 Fiber: 7.4 g, Total Sugars: 6.5 g, Potassium: 428 mg

My mother used to make this famous Arabian dish for me when I was a kid. It has incredible variations because tomatoes are delicious on their own and combined with many different ingredients. In this recipe, I suggest roasted tomatoes with garlic and Italian herbs. Sometimes I drizzle them with balsamic vinegar, but I also often cook them with shredded parmesan/ mozzarella or crumbled feta cheese. I use leftovers for bruschetta, toasted sandwiches, pasta toppings, or salads.

ROASTED TOMATOES

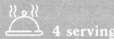 4 servings  5 minutes  10 minutes

INGREDIENTS:

- 4-5 ripe small tomatoes, halved
- olive oil/avocado oil spray
- 6 garlic cloves, finely chopped
- ½ tsp. red pepper flakes
- ¼ tsp. kosher salt
- a bunch of fresh thyme, basil, oregano, chopped

STEPS:

1. Spray tomato halves with avocado oil and season with salt and red pepper.
2. Preheat your air fryer to 350°F (180°C). Place the tomatoes in the basket in a single layer. Cook for 8 minutes. Also, you can arrange the tomatoes in a pan and put the pan into the air fryer.
3. Sprinkle the tomato halves with chopp.

EACH SERVING HAS:

Calories: 58, Carbs: 6 g, Chol: 0 mg, Sodium: 6 mg, Fat: 3.7 g, Protein: 1.2 Fiber: 1.4 g, Total Sugars: 2.5 g, Potassium: 249 mg

FISH & SEAFOOD

My dad likes to say that salmon is hard to ruin. This versatile fish is loved far and wide, not only in the Mediterranean. You don't need anything extra to enjoy it — it is delicious on its own. Therefore, take care to choose a garnish with a gentle flavor. And most importantly, do not go overboard with herbs and spices.

Salmon with a refreshing salad is a quick and easy dish for a weeknight dinner. Don't marinate salmon for over 15 minutes because it can become tough and over-salted. If you are using frozen fish, defrost before marinating and arrange the salmon fillets in a single layer in the air fryer basket.

Lemon marinade can be substituted for garlic butter marinade. The cooking steps are the same. Serve it with baked potato, pasta, or lemon garlic broccoli.

AIR-FRIED SALMON WITH SALAD

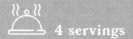 4 servings 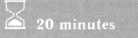 20 minutes 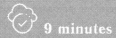 9 minutes

INGREDIENTS:

- 4 salmon fillets (180 g each) skin-on/skinless
- lime wedges for sprinkling

FOR THE MARINADE
- 1 Tbsp. extra virgin olive oil
- ½ big lemon, juiced
- 2 garlic cloves, crushed
- ½ tsp. dried rosemary
- ½ tsp. dried thyme
- ¼ tsp. smoked paprika
- a pinch of salt and pepper

FOR THE SALAD
- 2 avocados, peeled and chopped
- 3 tomatoes (400 g), chopped
- 1 red onion (70 g), chopped
- 2 Tbsp. drained capers
- 2 Tbsp. olive oil
- 1 Tbsp. white wine vinegar
- 1 Tbsp. fresh lemon juice
- ½ tsp. dried oregano
- 1 Tbsp. fresh parsley, chopped
- a pinch of sea salt and pepper

STEPS:

1. Combine all the ingredients for the marinade and cover the salmon fillets with it. Let the salmon rest in the fridge for 15 minutes.
2. Use olive oil spray for an air fryer. Place the salmon fillets skin side down into a preheated to 400°F (205°C) air fryer for 8 minutes.
3. In a bowl, combine all the ingredients for the salad.
4. Serve this flaky salmon with the salad and lime wedges.

EACH SERVING HAS:

Calories: 570, Carbs: 17 g, Chol: 78 mg, Sodium: 221 mg, Fat: 41.7 g, Protein: 38 g, Fiber: 9.4 g, Total Sugars: 4.5 g, Potassium: 1477 mg

People in Spain and Greece love the healthy combination of white fish and seasonal vegetables. Our family also loves it. The main thing in this dish is not to overcook the fish so that it remains moist inside with a light golden crust. Adjust the cooking time according to the thickness of the fish fillets — even 1 extra minute can change the texture. The crunchiness of the vegetables only accentuates the juiciness of the white fish.

I love the lemon-garlic flavor of this white fish, but you can replace the seasoning with curry, paprika, or Italian herbs. Seasoning the fish with aromatic marjoram, lemon zest, and salt will make this dish very Mediterranean. You can use air fryer parchment liners to keep the fish from sticking.

WHITE FISH

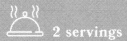 2 servings    5 minutes    25 minutes

INGREDIENTS:

- 2 cod/hake/tilapia/haddock fillets (6 oz./170 g each), 1-inch thickness

FOR THE RUB
- ½ tsp. garlic powder
- ½ tsp. onion powder
- 1 Tbsp. fresh lemon juice
- a pinch of sea salt
- olive oil spray

FOR THE SALAD
- ½ red/yellow/white onion (40 g), cut into strips
- 1 small bell pepper (110 g), wedges
- 1 baby potato, diced
- 4 cherry tomatoes
- 2 Tbsp. olive oil
- salt, and pepper to taste

STEPS:

1. Mix all rub ingredients.
2. Slightly drizzle the fish fillets with olive oil. Rub the fish with the garlic-onion mixture.
3. Spray an air fryer basket with olive oil. Arrange the fillets in a single layer in the basket.
4. Cook for 7-10 minutes in the air fryer that has been preheated to 360°F (180°C).
5. Toss vegetables with olive oil, salt, and pepper and spread them in a single layer in the basket.
6. Cook for 10-13 minutes in the air fryer that has been preheated to 400°F (205°C). Flip vegetables every 5 minutes.
7. Serve the fish with the vegetables, drizzled with lime juice.

EACH SERVING HAS:

Calories: 346, Carbs: 19.9 g, Chol: 83 mg, Sodium: 122 mg, Fat: 16.2 g, Protein: 33.8 g, Fiber: 4.4 g, Total Sugars: 11.5 g, Potassium: 747 mg

This recipe combines some of your favorite Mediterranean ingredients: tuna, parmesan, Greek yogurt, and Italian herbs. My kids love eating these patties as a snack, but they're also great for a hearty lunch with rice, fresh vegetables, and sauce. Sometimes I set aside some breadcrumbs and cheese and roll each patty in them for a yummy crunchy crust.

I also recommend adding various vegetables, such as very finely chopped bell peppers and red onions or grated carrots.

Uncooked or cooked patties can be stored in the freezer for up to 2 months.

TUNA PATTIES

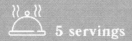 5 servings    10 minutes   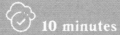 10 minutes

INGREDIENTS:

- 2 (5 oz./140 g each) cans tuna, drained and shredded
- 1 garlic clove, crushed
- ½ cup (60 g) Parmesan, finely shredded
- 1 cup (150 g) breadcrumbs
- ¼ cup (30 g) feta cheese/Mozzarella, crumbled
- 2 medium eggs, slightly beaten
- ½ lime, juice, and zest
- 2 Tbsp. Greek yogurt
- 2 Tbsp. olive oil
- 2 Tbsp. Dijon mustard
- 1 tsp. Italian herbs/paprika/oregano
- a pinch of salt and black pepper
- 2 Tbsp. basil, chopped

STEPS:

1. Combine all the ingredients in a large bowl and mix well.
2. Preheat the air fryer to 350°F (180°C) and line the basket with parchment paper.
3. Form tuna into 5 cakes using your hands. Arrange them in the basket and cook for 10 minutes until deep golden brown.

EACH SERVING HAS:

Calories: 311, Carbs: 24.1 g, Chol: 88 mg, Sodium: 524 mg, Fat: 15.2 g, Protein: 19.4 g, Fiber: 1.8 g, Total Sugars: 2.5 g, Potassium: 209 mg

The combination of shrimp with lime and garlic is already a classic. I always used to pan-fry them before I had the air fryer, but the air fryer gives them a golden, crispy crust and keeps them moist inside. I simply increase the cooking time by 3-4 minutes if I am starting with frozen shrimp.

I serve them in a sauce with pasta, rice, and beans, as an ingredient in a salad or cocktail, as an appetizer, or simply as a separate dish. They are very nutritious and hearty.

GARLIC SHRIMP WITH LEMON

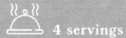 4 servings   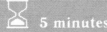 5 minutes    10 minutes

INGREDIENTS:

- 1 lb. (450 g) raw shrimp, peeled and deveined
- 2 garlic cloves, minced
- ½ tsp. anise seeds
- 1 Tbsp. olive oil
- a pinch of sea salt, and black pepper
- 2 Tbsp. fresh parsley, finely chopped
- 4 lime wedges for sprinkling

STEPS:

1. Preheat your air fryer to 400°F (205°C).
2. Toss shrimp with garlic, anise seeds, olive oil, salt, and pepper.
3. Arrange shrimp in a single layer in an air fryer basket. Cook for 10-12 minutes, depending on the size of the shrimp.
4. Sprinkle with chopped parsley and serve with lime wedges.

EACH SERVING HAS:

Calories: 173, Carbs: 4.1 g, Chol: 237 mg, Sodium: 276 mg, Fat: 5.2 g, Protein: 26 g, Fiber: 0.8 g, Total Sugars: 0.5 g, Potassium: 228 mg

For almost any quick meal, the scallops should be dry. Only then will you get a delicious golden crust. Be careful not to overcook them because they become rubbery.

Scallops are great as a snack or as an appetizer. They are high in calories, so I prefer a light garnish. I also like to serve them with air fried asparagus, zucchini noodles, spaghetti, rice, or orzo pasta.

ORANGE BASIL SCALLOPS

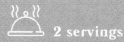 2 servings    7 minutes    7 minutes

INGREDIENTS:

- 8 sea scallops
- 1 garlic clove, minced
- 1 tsp. orange/lemon juice
- 2 Tbsp. basil, chopped
- 2 Tbsp. olive oil/salted butter, melted
- a pinch of sea salt and pepper
- 1 pinch of red pepper flakes
- oil spray

STEPS:

1. Preheat your air fryer to 400°F (205°C). Coat the basket lightly using an oil spray.
2. Season scallops with salt and pepper and sprinkle with olive oil.
3. Arrange them in a single layer in an air fryer basket. Cook for 5-7 minutes, depending on the size of the scallops, flipping them once.
4. Combine orange juice, red pepper flakes, chopped basil, olive oil, salt, and pepper.
5. Serve scallops with the orange dressing and asparagus or zucchini.

EACH SERVING HAS:

Calories: 289, Carbs: 3.5 g, Chol: 40 mg, Sodium: 194 mg, Fat: 22 g, Protein: 20.3 g, Fiber: 0.1 g, Total Sugars: 0.1 g, Potassium: 403 mg

POULTRY & MEAT

This dish is a lifesaver for moms of school kids. On school nights, my kids need an incredibly tasty, nutritious, quick-to-make, and meaty dish. These Greek chicken thighs are perfect. I leave them to marinate overnight and then pop them in the air fryer. In 20 minutes, the mouthwatering chicken pieces are ready, and there is no need to fire up the grill.

As a side dish, my foodies love rice, Mediterranean salad, or mashed potato. These thighs are so juicy and flavorful that my kids don't even ask for dessert after them and have forgotten about KFC. And I eat up what's left over, if there is any leftover, of course.

GREEK CHICKEN THIGHS

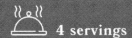 4 servings   4 minutes    20 minutes

(plus ½-8 hours for marinating)

INGREDIENTS:

- 4 chicken thighs, bone-in and skin-on
- 1 lemon, juice and zest
- 1 Tbsp. dried rosemary
- 4 garlic cloves, minced
- a pinch of sea salt and black pepper
- 1 Tbsp. Balsamic vinegar
- 1 Tbsp. olive oil
- lemon wedges for garnish

STEPS:

1. Combine olive oil, lemon juice, zest, rosemary, salt, and pepper. Brush over the chicken thighs and let them marinate for at least 2 hours.
2. Preheat your air fryer to 380°F (195°C). Coat the basket lightly using an oil spray.
3. Arrange chicken thighs in the basket skin side down. Cook for 15-20 minutes, flipping two times.
4. Sprinkle with lemon juice and serve with pesto sauce.

EACH SERVING HAS:

Calories: 404, Carbs: 3.6 g, Chol: 140 mg, Sodium: 129 mg, Fat: 29.2 g, Protein: 30.3 g, Fiber: 1 g, Total Sugars: 0.6 g, Potassium: 53 mg

It's hard to get respect and approval from my teenage children, but these souvlakis have bailed me out more than once. Even their friends like them. These crispy kebabs are a great addition to a picnic or small teen party. They came to us from Greek street food.

Sometimes I add veggies that I have on hand to the skewered chicken. The souvlaki only benefits from this. You can also replace chicken with pork, beef, or lamb pieces. In that case, you need to increase the cooking time a little bit and not ignore the marinating stage.

Many Mediterranean dishes are suitable for the keto diet, like these souvlakis, for example.

CHICKEN SOUVLAKI

 8 servings

 10 minutes
(plus 1-8 hours for marinating)

 15 minutes

INGREDIENTS:

- 2 lb. (900 g) chicken fillets, cut into 2-inch cubes
- 1 Tbsp. dried thyme
- 2 Tbsp. olive oil
- 4 garlic cloves, minced
- 1 tsp. sea salt
- 1 tsp. smoked paprika
- ½ tsp. ground white peppercorns
- ¼ tsp. red pepper flakes
- ½ lemon, juiced

STEPS:

1. Combine olive oil, lemon juice, herbs, spices, salt, and minced garlic.
2. Marinate chicken bites in the spice oil mix for 1-2 hours.
3. Thread the chicken pieces onto the skewers.
4. Preheat the air fryer to 400°F (204°C). Line the basket with parchment paper.
5. Arrange the skewers in the basket and cook for 15 minutes, flipping after the first 7 minutes.
6. Serve souvlaki with pita bread, tzatziki sauce, and tomato salad.

EACH SERVING HAS:

Calories: 249, Carbs: 2.1 g, Chol: 100 mg, Sodium: 110 mg, Fat: 11.9 g, Protein: 32.8 g, Fiber: 0.4 g, Total Sugars: 0.2 g, Potassium: 293 mg

Stuffed chicken is excellent for a weeknight dinner, and don't worry, it's quick and easy to make. In fact, you can choose any kind of filling for the chicken breast. The mozzarella can be replaced with feta cheese, cream cheese, or goat cheese (choose a soft cheese, so it's not rubbery when it cools). And the sun-dried tomatoes can be replaced with chopped spinach or roasted mushrooms.

Cold breasts can be sliced as an appetizer, but I like to eat them warm with melted cheese. Air-fried baby potatoes, crispy asparagus, or mashed cauliflower would work as a side dish.

STUFFED CHICKEN BREAST

 2 servings   5 minutes   40 minutes

INGREDIENTS:

- 2 chicken breasts
- 4 oz. (110 g) mozzarella/feta cheese, shredded
- 4 sun-dried tomatoes, chopped
- 8 black olives, diced
- 1 Tbsp. oregano
- a pinch of sea salt and pepper
- olive oil spray

STEPS:

1. Cut the chicken breasts horizontally, making a pocket.
2. Mix shredded mozzarella, sun-dried tomatoes, chopped olives, oregano, salt, and pepper.
3. Fill the chicken pockets with mozzarella stuffing and spray with olive oil.
4. Cook in the air fryer for 32-37 minutes at 400°F (204°C). Flip once halfway.

EACH SERVING HAS:

Calories: 403, Carbs: 12.7 g, Chol: 136 mg, Sodium: 361 mg, Fat: 17.4 g, Protein: 49.4 g, Fiber: 4.4 g, Total Sugars: 6.6 g, Potassium: 1362 mg

I love to eat air-fried meat and poultry, but it always needs some sauce, dip, or dressing. In this recipe, I cook the chicken breasts in the air fryer and make the sauce on the stovetop. Simmering them together for 10 minutes allows the chicken to soak up the creamy mushroom sauce. The chicken breast comes out with the perfect texture and makes one dish along with the sauce.

This dish is great for keto and paleo diets — no need to substitute ingredients for low-carb ones. It tastes even better the next.

CREAMY CHICKEN WITH MUSHROOMS

 4 servings 5 minutes 30 minutes

INGREDIENTS:

- 4 chicken breasts
- 2 Tbsp. leek, chopped
- 4 Tbsp. salted butter
- 4 oz. (110 g) mushrooms, diced
- 4 oz. (110 g) spinach, chopped
- 4 oz. (110 g) parmesan, shredded
- 1 cup (240 ml) heavy cream/high-fat milk/Greek yogurt
- 2 garlic cloves, crushed
- a pinch of sea salt and ground white pepper
- olive oil spray

STEPS:

1. Preheat your air fryer to 400⁰F (204⁰C).
2. Season chicken breasts with salt and pepper. Arrange them in the basket and cook for 20 minutes, flipping halfway through.
3. In a skillet, melt the butter. Add chopped leeks, mushrooms, and crushed garlic, and sauté for 5-7 minutes.
4. Add spinach and continue stirring occasionally. Add heavy cream and shredded parmesan.
5. Dip the cooked chicken breasts into the sauce and let them simmer gently for 10 minutes.
6. Serve with rice, spaghetti, or pasta.

EACH SERVING HAS:

Calories: 647, Carbs: 5.7 g, Chol: 230 mg, Sodium: 461 mg, Fat: 50.9 g, Protein: 43.4 g, Fiber: 1 g, Total Sugars: 0.6 g, Potassium: 856 mg

TURKEY MEATBALLS

Meatballs can be pan-fried, baked in the oven, or stewed with sauce. If you fry them, they absorb a lot of oil and become less healthy. If you bake them in the oven, they get very dry inside. That's why I really like to cook them in an air fryer — they get juicy on the inside and crispy on the outside. Moreover, we use a minimal amount of oil.

If you don't like sun-dried tomatoes, you can replace them with smoked paprika or red pepper flakes. Meatballs go well with hummus, tzatziki sauce, or baba ganoush.

TURKEY MEATBALLS

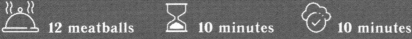

12 meatballs   10 minutes   10 minutes

INGREDIENTS:

- 1 lb. (450 g) ground turkey
- 1 cup (60 g) fresh spinach, chopped
- 4 oz. (110 g) feta/mozzarella, shredded
- 2 sun-dried tomatoes, chopped
- ½ red onion, chopped
- 2 garlic cloves, minced
- 1 medium egg, slightly beaten
- ¼ cup (40 g) breadcrumbs
- 1 tsp. fresh rosemary, chopped
- a pinch of sea salt

STEPS:

1. Thoroughly combine all the ingredients in a bowl.
2. Use your hands to shape small meatballs from the mixture. Arrange them in a lightly oiled air fryer basket in a single layer.
3. Cook at 400°F (204°C) for 10-15 minutes, depending on the size of the meatballs. Flip them halfway through.
4. Serve with tzatziki dip or baba ganoush.

EACH SERVING HAS:

Calories: 124, Carbs: 4.7 g, Chol: 60 mg, Sodium: 177 mg, Fat: 6.9 g, Protein: 12.4 g, Fiber: 0.7 g, Total Sugars: 1.6 g, Potassium: 205 mg

LAMB CHOPS

Lamb chops are a holiday dish in our family and for a good reason. They are pretty easy to make and can keep for a long time. In this recipe, I put together a mix of my favorite Mediterranean spices for the marinade. I'm sure you'll love them too.

Classic side dishes for lamb chops are lemon garlic roasted asparagus, glazed carrots, green beans, and Greek salad. Who are we to argue with haute cuisine?! We obey completely and cook them all one at a time. Incredibly delicious and very Mediterranean!

LAMB CHOPS

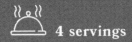 4 servings   10 minutes
(1 hour-overnight-marinating time)   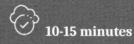 10-15 minutes

INGREDIENTS:

- 8 lamb chops 1½ lb. (700 g)

FOR THE MARINADE:

- 2 Tbsp. avocado oil/ghee
- 2 Tbsp. Greek yogurt
- 2 garlic cloves, minced
- 1 tsp. smoked paprika
- 1 tsp. coriander powder
- 1 tsp. allspice
- ¼ chili pepper
- 1 tsp. fresh lemon juice
- ½ tsp. lemon zest
- ½ tsp. sea salt
- ½ tsp. ground white pepper

STEPS:

1. Combine all the ingredients for the marinade.
2. Brush lamb chops with the marinade mixture and let them rest for 1-2 hours.
3. Arrange chops in a single layer in an air fryer basket.
4. Preheat your air fryer to 400°F (204°C).
   Cook for 8 minutes for medium-rare and 12 minutes for medium-well. Flip halfway through.
5. Serve with green peas, cauliflower rice, or air-fried potato wedges.

EACH SERVING HAS:

Calories: 327, Carbs: 1.4 g, Chol: 113 mg, Sodium: 123 mg, Fat: 18.5 g, Protein: 35.4 g, Fiber: 0.3 g, Total Sugars: 0.4 g, Potassium: 36 mg

PORK TENDERLOIN

I really love it when we have guests over. We talk a lot, eat delicious food, and play games. I always come up with some interesting recipes for these occasions that are so dear to my heart.

Before I had my own family to cook for, I would cook special meals just for my friends. Initially, I fiddled with complicated recipes, and I would cook all day or even longer. Over time, I discovered unique and delicious recipes but slightly easier to make. And now that my hustle and bustle has multiplied, I can still delight my "nears and dears" with something special. And let them guess what it is and how I made it. I will tell only you, my dear readers. Air Fried Pork Tenderloin is one of those rare finds.

PORK TENDERLOIN

 2 servings   5 minutes   20 minutes

INGREDIENTS:

- 1 lb. (450 g) pork tenderloin, cut into 2 pieces
- 3 garlic cloves, minced
- 1 Tbsp. Dijon mustard
- 1 Tbsp. oregano
- a pinch of sea salt, and ground white pepper

STEPS:

1. Combine all the ingredients, except the tenderloin, in a small bowl.
2. Slice the pork tenderloin but not all the way through (make small slits in the top about 1 inch apart).
3. Preheat your air fryer to 400°F (204°C).
4. Spread the mustard mixture over the pork, completely covering the top. Arrange the coated tenderloins in the basket.
5. Cook for 20 minutes.

EACH SERVING HAS:

Calories: 341, Carbs: 3.4 g, Chol: 164 mg, Sodium: 218 mg, Fat: 8.5 g, Protein: 59.4 g, Fiber: 1.3 g, Total Sugars: 0.2 g, Potassium: 1014 mg

Usually, I like to cook pork chops bone-in because the meat comes out juicy with a crispy crust. But in this recipe, even boneless pieces turn out moist inside, thanks to the cheese coating and quick cooking at high temperatures.

You can add breadcrumbs to the cheese mixture or make them completely breaded. If you have thicker chops, just increase the cooking time by a few minutes. The crust should be golden brown but not too dry. And be careful with the salt because the cheese is already salty.

As a side dish, my husband likes spinach, air-fried onion and garlic, green beans, or wild rice.

PORK WITH CHEESE CRISP

 4 servings  5 minutes 13 minutes

INGREDIENTS:

- 4 pork chops (5 oz./140 g each, 1-inch thick), boneless
- ½ cup (60 g) parmesan/cheddar cheese, shredded
- 2 garlic cloves, minced
- 2 Tbsp. avocado oil (optional)
- ¼ tsp. sea salt (optional)
- 1 tsp. onion powder
- 1 tsp. red pepper flakes
- ¼ tsp. ground white pepper

STEPS:

1. Brush pork chops with avocado oil.
2. Mix shredded cheese with spices, minced garlic, and salt. Cover the pork chops with the cheese mixture.
3. Place them in an air fryer basket in a single layer. Cook at 390°F (200°C) for 13 minutes, flipping the pork halfway through.
4. Serve with potato hash, air-fried asparagus, or wild rice.

EACH SERVING HAS:

Calories: 320, Carbs: 2.4 g, Chol: 80 mg, Sodium: 196 mg, Fat: 24.5 g, Protein: 23.4 g, Fiber: 0.3 g, Total Sugars: 0.3 g, Potassium: 320 mg

BEEF KOFTA KEBAB

This delicious and simple dish came to us from Lebanon and Turkey. Initially, it was cooked on a grill, but we have converted it to an air fryer. It has caught on so well with us because of its versatility. It keeps well in the fridge for 3 to 4 days. And it can be used for ready-to-eat lunches, snacks, and appetizers.

My family loves these spicy meatballs because they resemble street food but can be made quickly at home. Instead of the spices I recommend, you can use any ready-made Middle Eastern blend you like — Greek, Turkish, or Lebanese. I recommend baba ganoush, tzatziki sauce, and hummus as sides.

BEEF KOFTA KEBAB

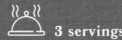 3 servings   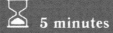 5 minutes    10 minutes

INGREDIENTS:

- ½ lb. (225 g) ground beef/lamb
- 1 garlic clove, minced
- 1 small red onion (50 g), finely chopped
- ¼ tsp. nutmeg
- ¼ tsp. allspice
- ¼ tsp. paprika
- ⅛ tsp. ground black pepper
- ¼ tsp. cumin
- ¼ tsp. cardamom
- ¼ tsp. sea salt

STEPS:

1. Thoroughly combine all the ingredients.
2. Form 6 oval koftas by hand. If you prefer, you can string the meat on skewers.
3. Place the koftas in an air fryer basket in a single layer. Cook at 350°F (178°C) for 12 minutes, flipping halfway through.
4. Serve kofta kebabs with pita bread and air-fried veggies.

EACH SERVING HAS:

Calories: 157, Carbs: 3 g, Chol: 67 mg, Sodium: 51 mg, Fat: 4.5 g, Protein: 23.2 g, Fiber: 0.7 g, Total Sugars: 1.1 g, Potassium: 352 mg

Honestly, I bought an air fryer to cook quickly and without burning. That's why I use it for cooking whole dishes and frying semi-finished ingredients for more complex dishes. After all, the same result can be achieved in the oven, in a pan, or on the grill. But with an air fryer, you are guaranteed to get meat that is juicy on the inside and has a lightly crispy crust. This perfect combination is difficult to achieve any other way — especially if you're distracted by talking on the phone, as I often am.

Here I present to you air-fried beef short ribs. With this recipe, you will no longer hesitate to make them. And it's the healthiest way to cook beef.

BEEF SHORT RIBS

 3 servings 5 minutes
(plus 1-8 hours for marinating)
 16 minutes

INGREDIENTS:

- 1 lb. (450 g) beef short ribs

FOR THE MARINADE:
- 4 Tbsp. olive oil
- ¼ cup (60 ml) white wine vinegar
- ⅛ tsp. Worcestershire sauce
- 2 garlic cloves, diced
- ⅓ cup (20 g) fresh rosemary, chopped
- ¼ cup (15 g) fresh thyme, chopped
- ¼ tsp. sea salt

STEPS:

1. Mix together all the ingredients for the marinade.
2. Brush beef ribs with the marinade and refrigerate for at least 1 hour.
3. Arrange the ribs in an air fryer basket in a single layer. Cook at 400°F (204°C) for 16 minutes, flipping halfway through (brush with extra marinade).
4. Serve with Burgundy mushroom sauce, marinara sauce, or garlic herb butter sauce.

EACH SERVING HAS:

Calories: 507, Carbs: 7.5 g, Chol: 137 mg, Sodium: 107 mg, Fat: 33.5 g, Protein: 44.2 g, Fiber: 4.3 g, Total Sugars: 0.2 g, Potassium: 661 mg

DESSERTS

My kids really love these Italian cookies. They are crunchy but not too hard. They enjoy them with tea, milk, or milkshakes. If the biscotti unintentionally get very hard, they soak them in milk or yogurt, like granola.

I've given a basic recipe here, but feel free to make your variations. Instead of anise, you can add orange zest, cinnamon, or cardamom for flavor. Choosing soft berries and nuts is better, as they do not make the cookies too hard. The biscotti are more delicate when made with butter than with olive oil.

ITALIAN BISCOTTI

 4 servings   15 minutes   12 minutes

INGREDIENTS:

- 1 cup (130 g) all-purpose flour
- ⅓ cup (80 g) white sugar
- 2 medium eggs
- 3 Tbsp. olive oil
- 1 tsp. vanilla extract
- 1 tsp. anise extract
- 1 tsp. baking powder
- cranberries, chopped pistachios (optional)
- olive oil spray, for the air fryer basket

STEPS:

1. Mix all the ingredients for the batter. Shape into a flat loaf.
2. Lightly coat an air fryer basket with olive oil and preheat to 320°F (160°C).
3. Place the loaf into the basket and cook for 7 minutes.
4. Cool the loaf for 10 minutes and slice it into 1-inch pieces.
5. Arrange the slices in the air fryer basket and cook for 5 minutes at 320°F (160°C).
6. Store in a glass jar.

EACH SERVING HAS:

Calories: 355, Carbs: 46.1 g, Chol: 82 mg, Sodium: 38 mg, Fat: 17 g, Protein: 6.2 g, Fiber: 1.1 g, Total Sugars: 20.2 g, Potassium: 205 mg

STUFFED BAKED APPLES

The warmest memories from my childhood are the smell of warm pastries and baked apples. They have been with me all my life. These memories allow me to hide and come to my senses when life shows me its unpleasant side. Maybe this recipe will help you that way, too. So, to-die-for and straightforward!

The toppings and spices can be substituted with your favorites or to suit your mood. You can make these baked apples at least every day. They require a whole hour in the oven, but in the air fryer, they are ready in 20 minutes. You can choose almost any kind of apple. If you cut them into halves, they will bake a little faster. If you don't like honey, you can replace it with brown sugar.

STUFFED BAKED APPLES

 **1 apple** 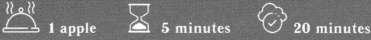 **5 minutes**   **20 minutes**

INGREDIENTS:

- 1 apple, cored, but leave a bottom

FOR THE STUFFING:
- 1 Tbsp. honey
- 1 tsp. unsalted butter
- 1 Tbsp. nuts, crushed
- 1 Tbsp. raisins/dried cranberries/ dried apricots
- 1 Tbsp. oats (optional)
- ⅛ tsp. cinnamon
- ⅛ tsp. cardamom

STEPS:

1. Mix all the ingredients for the stuffing. Spoon the stuffing into the hole in the apple.
2. Place the apple into the air fryer basket and cook for 20 minutes at 350^{0}F (180^{0}C).
3. Serve warm with a scoop of ice cream and caramel sauce.

EACH SERVING HAS:

Calories: 314, Carbs: 61.8 g, Chol: 10 mg, Sodium: 89 mg, Fat: 9 g, Protein: 3.2 g, Fiber: 7.7 g, Total Sugars: 46.2 g, Potassium: 393 mg

BANANA NUT BREAD

Banana bread is the kind of secret recipe that gets passed from grandmother to mother and from mother to daughter. And because we're afraid to break the generational continuity, we haven't changed anything for centuries. Except for the way we bake, of course. I'm the only one in our family who cooks it in an air fryer, and I'm already thinking about how to give it to my daughter. She likes it so much that I'm afraid she won't change anything about it either. Maybe she will just bake it in some Nano oven over the Internet!

BANANA NUT BREAD

 8 slices 10 minutes 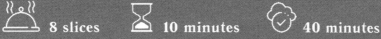 40 minutes

INGREDIENTS:

- ⅓ cup (80 ml) olive oil/unsalted butter, softened
- ½ cup (120 ml) liquid honey
- 2 whole eggs, slightly beaten
- 2 ripe bananas, mushed
- ⅔ cup (60 g) walnuts, chopped
- 3 chopped walnuts, for sprinkling
- 1¼ cup (170 g) all-purpose flour
- ½ tsp. ground cinnamon
- ¼ tsp. nutmeg
- ⅛ tsp. sea salt
- 1 tsp. baking powder

STEPS:

1. Combine all the ingredients using a mixer.
2. Pour the batter into a greased loaf pan that is the right size for the air fryer basket. You can use an 8"x 4" pan, but mini pans bake quicker.
3. Sprinkle chopped walnuts and some brown sugar on top.
4. Cook in the preheated air fryer at 330°F (165°C) for 25-40 minutes, checking with a toothpick for doneness.
5. Glaze with sugar-milk mix (optional).

EACH SERVING HAS:

Calories: 313, Carbs: 41.8 g, Chol: 41 mg, Sodium: 18 mg, Fat: 15.3 g, Protein: 5.8 g, Fiber: 2 g, Total Sugars: 21.2 g, Potassium: 258 mg

RASPBERRY CLAFOUTI

It's rare to find a dessert as quick and easy-to-cook as clafouti. Unfortunately, it doesn't keep very long, but the truth is you don't need it to. Your family will eat it faster. Clafouti is similar to a berry frittata. It needs time to cool, but it should definitely be eaten warm. That is: you want to catch the moment when the clafouti reveals its best texture to you, which is about half an hour to an hour after baking.

Celebrate summer with clafouti! I usually make clafouti with raspberries or cherries because my family likes it that way. But I've also tried it with blueberries, strawberries, and peaches. Try them all and choose your favorite.

RASPBERRY CLAFOUTI

 2 servings   7 minutes   30 minutes

INGREDIENTS:

- 3 Tbsp. all-purpose flour
- 1 large whole egg
- ¼ cup (60 ml) whole milk
- 2 Tbsp. light brown sugar
- ¼ tsp. vanilla extract
- 6 oz. (170 g) fresh raspberries/ cherries
- 1 pinch of sea salt
- powdered sugar for sprinkling

STEPS:

1. Preheat your air fryer to 320°F (160°C).
2. Grease a 6" baking dish with butter.
3. Place raspberries at the bottom of the dish.
4. Whisk together all the remaining ingredients and pour the mixture into the raspberries.
5. Bake for 30 minutes until golden brown.
6. Sprinkle with powdered sugar and serve.

EACH SERVING HAS:

Calories: 179, Carbs: 30.2 g, Chol: 96 mg, Sodium: 51 mg, Fat: 4.3 g, Protein: 6.4 g, Fiber: 5.9 g, Total Sugars: 15 g, Potassium: 231 mg

LEMON RICOTTA CAKE

This delicate Italian miracle comes together very quickly and consists of just a few ingredients, most of which are always on hand. The main secret here is to whip the dough well. The fluffier the dough, the more air it absorbs, and the lighter and more delicate the texture of the cooked pie. If you don't like the citrus flavor, you can skip the lemon zest altogether.

My kids like lemon cake with berry sauce (blueberries, raspberries, strawberries, etc.) and a cup of herbal tea.

LEMON RICOTTA CAKE

 6 servings   7 minutes 25 minutes

INGREDIENTS:

- 3 egg whites, whisked
- 3 egg yolks, at room temperature
- ⅛ tsp. sea salt
- ¾ cup (180 g) white sugar
- ½ tsp. vanilla extract
- 1 cup (250 g) unsalted butter, melted
- 1 cup (130 g) all-purpose flour
- 1 cup (250 g) whole-milk ricotta cheese
- 2 lemons zest
- 1 tsp. baking powder

STEPS:

1. Combine all the ingredients except the egg whites. Mix well using a mixer/food processor/blender. Carefully add whisked egg whites.
2. Preheat your air fryer to 320°F (160°C).
3. Spray a baking pan with olive oil and pour the batter into the pan.
4. Bake for 20-25 minutes, checking with a toothpick for doneness.
5. Serve warm or cold with a cup of coffee or herbal tea.

EACH SERVING HAS:

Calories: 583, Carbs: 50.2 g, Chol: 184 mg, Sodium: 324 mg, Fat: 39.3 g, Protein: 10.4 g, Fiber: 1.1 g, Total Sugars: 30.6 g, Potassium: 207 mg

TAHINI OATMEAL COOKIES

I try not to leave these cookies in a jar on the table because, before I know it, they're gone. I can only guess from the happy faces of my housemates who did it. But I can't stay upset with them because I know how delicious they are. They're impossible to resist, even if a healthy lunch is in the fridge.

The nutty flavor and aroma come from the tahini and walnuts. I love tahini so much that I add it to many meals. It increases the nutritional value and adds a nutty flavor. I also love that these cookies bake quickly — only 5 to 8 minutes. Store them at room temperature, covered tightly, so they don't dry out.

TAHINI OATMEAL COOKIES

 8 cookies   5 minutes   8 minutes

INGREDIENTS:

- ⅓ cup (85 g) tahini paste
- ¼ cup (60 ml) liquid honey
- 1 cup (85 g) oat flakes
- 2 Tbsp. all-purpose flour
- ¼ cup (40 g) chocolate chips
- ¼ cup (40 g) walnuts
- ¼ tsp. cinnamon
- ½ tsp. vanilla extract
- ⅛ tsp. sea salt

STEPS:

1. Combine all the ingredients in a bowl.
2. Preheat your air fryer to 350⁰F (180⁰C).
3. Divide the batter into 8 pieces. Form the cookies and arrange them in an air fryer basket lined with parchment paper.
4. Bake for 5-7 minutes until crisp.
5. Serve with tea, coffee, or milk.

EACH SERVING HAS:

Calories: 193, Carbs: 22.2 g, Chol: 1 mg, Sodium: 17 mg, Fat: 10.9 g, Protein: 5.1 g, Fiber: 2.7 g, Total Sugars: 11.6 g, Potassium: 133 mg

CANNOLI

This Sicilian pastry is a festive dish. It takes a little bit of work to prepare, but the result is worth it. The air fryer makes it easier because you don't have to keep track of the shells. In exactly 5 minutes, they will be ready. You need special cylindrical baking molds to make the cannoli into the right shape. If you don't have molds, you can use aluminum foil. And be sure to spray everything with cooking spray — dough, molds, and air fryer basket.

Store the cannoli in the refrigerator. Be aware that they will soften and lose their crispy texture if you store them already filled. I like to dip them in hot chocolate after baking. Enjoy!

CANNOLI

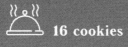 16 cookies   40 minutes   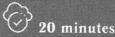 20 minutes

INGREDIENTS:

FOR THE DOUGH:

- 2 cups (260 g) all-purpose flour
- 2 tsp. white sugar
- ⅛ tsp. sea salt
- 2 Tbsp. cold butter, cubed
- 1 large egg yolk
- ½ cup (120 ml) dry white wine

FOR THE FILLING:

- 1 cup (250 g) ricotta cheese
- ⅔ cup (90 g) powdered sugar
- ½ tsp. cinnamon
- 1 cup (240 ml) heavy whipping cream, whipped

FOR DECORATING:

- ¼ cup (30 g) pistachios/walnuts/almonds, chopped
- ¼ cup (40 g) chocolate chips
- ¼ cup (40 g) dried fruits, finely chopped

STEPS:

1. Make crumbles from cold butter, flour, salt, and sugar. Add egg yolk and wine. Knead the dough and form it into a ball. Wrap the dough with plastic wrap and let it rest in the fridge for 30 minutes.
2. Mix ricotta, sugar, and ground cinnamon. Carefully combine the sweetened ricotta with whipped cream. Put the filling in the fridge until the shells are ready.
3. Preheat your air fryer to 400°F (205°C) and spray an air fryer basket with olive oil.
4. Take ¼ of the dough and make the first batch of shells. Roll out the dough to ⅛" thick. Using a cookie cutter, cut out four 4" circles.
5. Spray the circles with olive oil and roll around the cannoli forms.
6. Cook for 5 minutes until golden brown.
7. Repeat Steps 4 through 6 with the remaining dough.
8. Dip the shells into the chocolate, pour the filling inside, and sprinkle with chopped nuts or chocolate chips.
9. Store cannoli in the fridge. Assemble them just before serving if you want to keep them crispy.

EACH SERVING HAS:

Calories: 215, Carbs: 25 g, Chol: 43 mg, Sodium: 49 mg, Fat: 10.4 g, Protein: 4.6 g, Fiber: 0.7 g, Total Sugars: 9.6 g, Potassium: 87 mg

7-DAY MEAL PLAN

MONDAY

Breakfast	Mushroom Frittata 21
Lunch	Roasted Vegetables 47 + Chicken Souvlaki 77
Dinner	Air-Fried Salmon with Salad 63
Snacks	Roasted Almonds 35, Baba Ganoush with fresh vegetables 37

TUESDAY

Breakfast	Crispy Granola 23
Lunch	Stuffed Bell Peppers 51
Dinner	Garlic Shrimp with Lemon 69 + Greek Potatoes 49
Snacks	Asparagus with Tahini Sauce 53, Beef Kofta Kebab 91

WEDNESDAY

Breakfast	Egg Muffins 25
Lunch	Zucchini Salad 55 + Pork Tenderloin 87
Dinner	White Fish 65 + Roasted Tomatoes 59
Snacks	Falafel 39

THURSDAY

Breakfast	Mediterranean Toasts 27
Lunch	Crispy Cabbage 57 + Greek Chicken Thighs 75
Dinner	Tuna Patties 67
Snacks	Stuffed Mushrooms 41, Romesco Sauce 43

FRIDAY	
Breakfast	Breakfast Bowl 29
Lunch	Beef Short Ribs 93 + Crispy Greek Potatoes 49
Dinner	Orange Basil Scallops with mashed peas 71
Snacks	Tahini Oatmeal Cookies 107, Stuffed Mushrooms 41

SATURDAY	
Breakfast	French Toasts 31
Lunch	Lamb Chops 85 + Roasted Vegetables 47
Dinner	Creamy Chicken with Mushrooms 81
Snacks	Baba Ganoush 37

SUNDAY	
Breakfast	Banana Nut Bread 101
Lunch	Pork with Cheese Crisp 89 + Asparagus with Tahini Sauce 53
Dinner	Stuffed Chicken Breast 79
Snacks	Roasted Almonds 35, Stuffed Baked Apples 99

DESSERTS (OPTIONAL FOR DINNER OR AS AN ADDITIONAL SNACK)

Italian Biscotti 97

Raspberry Clafouti 103

Lemon Ricotta Cake 105

Cannoli 109

This meal plan provides nutritional variety and accommodates different types of meals. You can customize the portions according to your caloric needs and preferences. Also, remember to drink enough water and include fresh fruits and vegetables as additional snacks as needed.

CONVENTIONAL OVEN
TO AIR FRYER CONVERSION

	Cooking Temperature	Cooking Time
Conventional Oven	200^{0}F (95^{0}C)	30 min
Air Fryer	185^{0}F (100^{0}C)	24 min

COOKING TIMES

	Time, min	Temperature
Poultry		
Breasts, Legs, Thighs (bone-in)	25-30	380^{0}F /195^{0}C
Breasts (boneless), Wings	12	380^{0}F /195^{0}C
Drumsticks	20	370^{0}F /190^{0}C
Tenders	10	360^{0}F /180^{0}C
Whole Chicken	75	360^{0}F /180^{0}C
Meat		
Meatballs	8-10	380^{0}F /195^{0}C
Burger	18	370^{0}F /190^{0}C
Beefsteak	12	400^{0}F /205^{0}C
Pork Chops	12	400^{0}F /205^{0}C
Bacon	8	400^{0}F /205^{0}C
Sausages	15	380^{0}F (195^{0}C)
Lamb Chops	10	400^{0}F (205^{0}C)
Fish & Seafood		
Fish Fillet	10	400^{0}F /205^{0}C
Calamari	4	400^{0}F /205^{0}C
Scallops, Shrimp	6	400^{0}F /205^{0}C

	Time, min	Temperature
Vegetables		
Asparagus	5	400^{0}F /205^{0}C
Broccoli	6	400^{0}F /205^{0}C
Carrots	15	380^{0}F /195^{0}C
Mushrooms	5	400^{0}F /205^{0}C
Onion	10	400^{0}F /205^{0}C
Peppers	15	400^{0}F /205^{0}C
Potatoes	12	400^{0}F /205^{0}C
Tomatoes	4-10	400^{0}F /205^{0}C
Frozen Foods		
Onion Rings	8	400^{0}F /205^{0}C
Mozzarella Sticks	8	400^{0}F /205^{0}C
Chicken Nuggets	10	400^{0}F /205^{0}C
Breaded Shrimp	9	400^{0}F /205^{0}C
Fish Sticks	10	400^{0}F /205^{0}C

MY STORY

My name is Linda Gilmore. I am a food journalist and author. I am highly recognized for making culinary magic in my home kitchen. I am also a busy mom of two. This means I am always on the run and looking for any chance to save time and money. I am a foodie through and through at my core, and I have grown into an **advocate for the Mediterranean lifestyle**. With a passion for healthy living and first-hand knowledge of what it takes to stick to a successful lifestyle plan, I will guide you throughout this journey.

The Internet is full of all the information a person might need, but surfing for the right pieces takes a lot of time and effort. Looking for answers to my amateurish questions made me read through countless complex professional texts.

How much did I wish I'd had a book with simple step-by-step explanations? Perhaps, that is the main reason why I've written this one.

I hope this book lets you enjoy the Mediterranean lifestyle with your air fryer!

OUR RECOMMENDATIONS

Mediterranean Meal Prep Cookbook: Heart Healthy Recipe Ideas for Cooking Ahead and Saving Time

Mediterranean Cookbook for Two: Healthy Mediterranean Cooking for Couples, Roommates, and Partners

Copyright

Printed in Great Britain
by Amazon

38384897R00066